Macarons Cookbook

for Beginners

Simplified Recipes to Start Making the Best Macarons Ever

BY

MOLLY MILLS

License Notes

No part of this book may be copied, replicated, distributed, sold or shared without the express and written consent of the Author.

The ideas expressed in the book are for entertainment purposes. The Reader assumes all risk when following any guidelines and the Author accepts no responsibility if damages occur due to actions taken by the Reader.

An Amazing Offer for Buying My Book!

Thank you very much for purchasing my books! As a token of my appreciation, I would like to extend an amazing offer to you! When you have subscribed with your e-mail address, you will have the opportunity to get free and discounted e-books that will show up in your inbox daily. You will also receive reminders before an offer expires so you never miss out. With just little effort on your part, you will have access to the newest and most informative books at your fingertips. This is all part of the VIP treatment when you subscribe below.

SIGN ME UP: *https://molly.gr8.com*

Table of Contents

Delicious Macarons Recipes

AAAAAAAAAAAAAAAAAAAAAAAAAAAAAAAAAAAAAAAAAAAAAAAAAAAA

Chapter I - Fruit Mania

To increase the nutritional value of macarons, add fruits of your choice. Here are some recipes you can start with!

ΛΛΛΛΛΛΛΛΛΛΛΛΛΛΛΛΛΛΛΛΛΛΛΛΛΛΛΛΛΛΛΛΛΛΛΛΛΛΛΛΛΛΛΛΛΛΛΛΛΛΛΛΛΛΛΛΛ

Recipe 1: Green Apple Macarons

As the saying goes, an apple a day, keeps the doctor away. If you don't like apples, give this recipe a try and fulfill your nutritional needs. You're going to love these apple based macarons.

Yield: 12

Cooking Time: 40 minutes

List of Ingredients:

For Macarons

- 2 egg whites
- White sugar, 250 grams
- Icing sugar, 200 grams
- Almond flour, 200 grams

For Frosting

- Apple jam, 3 ounces
- Vanilla essence, 1 teaspoon
- White sugar, ¾ cup
- 1 egg white

AA

Instructions:

Preheat the oven to 300 degrees.

In a food processor, mix almond flour and icing sugar.

In another bowl whisk 2 egg whites on medium speed.

Add white sugar and keep whisking to form a smooth glossy mixture.

Form macarons from the batter and bake for about 20 minutes.

Meanwhile, whisk the remaining egg white in a bowl.

Add white sugar and keep whisking.

Stir in apple jam and vanilla essence and whisk on medium speed for 3 minutes.

Refrigerate the frosting for 20 minutes.

Coat the freshly baked macarons with apple frosting and enjoy!

Recipe 2: Raspberry Macarons

Raspberries have a very distinct flavor. If you like experimenting with food, you would surely love this recipe. Mixing cream of tartar and raspberry jam really elevates the taste of this recipe.

Yield: 35

Cooking Time: 35minutes

List of Ingredients:

- Confectioner's sugar, 1 cup
- Raspberry jam, ¾ cup
- Almond flour, ¾ cup
- Purple food color, 3 to 4 drops
- Freshly made raspberry puree,
- 2 egg whites
- Powdered sugar, ¼ cup
- Cream of tartar, a pinch

AAAAAAAAAAAAAAAAAAAAAAAAAAAAAAAAAAAAAAAAAAAAAAAAAAAA

Instructions:

Preheat oven to 375 degrees.

Mix almond flour and sugar in a mixer on medium speed.

In a small bowl, whisk egg whites until fluffy.

Stir in powdered sugar and cream of tartar and whisk on medium speed for 3 minutes.

Add powdered mixture to whisked eggs and fold well using a spatula.

Form round macarons from the batter and bake for 20 minutes until golden brown.

Meanwhile, start preparing for the raspberry filling.

In a bowl, whisk raspberry puree and jam together to form a well-blended mixture.

Refrigerate for 10 minutes.

Take out the baked macarons and enjoy with chilled raspberry filling.

Recipe 3: Strawberry Macarons

Strawberry is almost everyone's favorite flavor! Give this recipe a try and see if you like strawberry flavored macrons. Their combination with coconut flakes really makes this recipe special.

Yield: 36

Cooking Time: 20min

List of Ingredients:

- Dried coconut flakes, 1 ½ cups
- Finely chopped strawberries (preferably dried), ½ cup
- Caster sugar, 1 cup
- Corn flour, 1 tablespoon
- 2 egg whites
- Food color (pink), 4-5 drops

AAAAAAAAAAAAAAAAAAAAAAAAAAAAAAAAAAAAAAAAAAAAAAAAAAAAA

Instructions:

Preheat oven to 150°C.

In a small sauce pan, whisk 1 egg white and stir in dried coconut.

Add ½ cup caster sugar to the mixture and mix all the ingredients well.

Add 2 tablespoons of distilled water to the mixture and heat over small flame.

When the sugar is completely dissolved, turn off the flame and allow the mixture to cool.

In another bowl, whisk the remaining white.

Add corn flour, remaining caster sugar and food color and whisk well.

Combine both mixtures together and whisk on medium speed for 3 minutes to form a thick batter.

Form small round macarons from the batter and bake for about 15 minutes until golden brown.

Enjoy with your favorite dip!

Recipe 4: Mango Macarons

Who doesn't love mangoes? While the fruit is used in pretty much everything; from ice-cream to pickles, it's time to try mango flavored macarons. You will definitely not regret trying this one!

Yield: 25

Cooking Time: 45 minutes

List of Ingredients:

For Macarons

- Powdered sugar, 1 cup
- Yellow food color, 2-4 drops
- Finely grounded almonds, ½ cup
- Lemon extract, 1 teaspoon
- Dried lemon zest, 1 teaspoon
- White sugar, 7 tablespoons
- 2 egg whites

For Mango Filling

- Fresh mango puree, ½ cup
- Unsalted butter, 2 tablespoons
- Lemon juice, 2tbsp
- Corn flour, 2 tablespoons
- Cooking salt, a pinch
- 2 egg yolks

AAAAAAAAAAAAAAAAAAAAAAAAAAAAAAAAAAAAAAAAAAAAAAAAAAAAAAAA

Instructions:

Preheat the oven to 300 degrees.

Mix lemon zest, almonds and powdered sugar in a food processor over medium speed to form a powdery mixture.

In a small bowl, whisk egg whites until fluffy.

Add white sugar gradually and keep whisking over medium speed to form a glossy mixture.

Combine both mixtures and fold well using a spatula.

Form small cookies from the batter and bake for about 15 minutes.

Meanwhile, whisk egg yolks in a small bowl.

Stir in lemon juice, mango puree, salt and corn flour and whisk some more.

In a small pan, heat butter over small flame.

When the butter is fully melted, add it to the rest of ingredients.

Whisk all the ingredients well and refrigerate for 20 minutes.

Enjoy freshly baked macarons with mango filing.

Recipe 5: Apricot Macarons

This is undoubtedly one of the healthiest macaron recipes. If you want to enjoy flawless skin, include these macarons in your daily diet. Apricots are known to improve skin.

Yield: 12

Cooking Time: 45minutes

List of Ingredients:

For Macaroons

- Coarsely chopped desiccated apricots, ½ cup
- Condensed milk, ¼ cup
- Coconut flakes (unsweetened), 1 ½ cups
- Vanilla beans, grounded (or paste), ½ teaspoons
- 1 large egg white

For Apricot Filling

- Caster sugar, ½ cup
- Fresh cream, 250g
- 1 lemon juice
- Greek yogurt, 1 ½ cups
- Orange blossom water, 2 teaspoons
- 6 apricots, coarsely chopped

AAAAAAAAAAAAAAAAAAAAAAAAAAAAAAAAAAAAAAAAAAAAAAAAAAAA

Instructions:

Preheat oven to 160°C.

In a small bowl whisk egg white until fluffy and set aside.

In another bowl, mix shredded coconut and condensed milk.

Finally, add vanilla paste to the mixture and combine all ingredients well.

Pour egg white into the mixture and whisk on medium speed to form a consistent batter.

Form small round macarons from the batter and bake for about 20 minutes.

While the macarons are baking, start preparing for the apricot filling.

In a small saucepan, mix lemon juice, sugar and 2/3 of diced apricots.

Heat the ingredients over small flame until the sugar is fully dissolved.

Add orange blossom water and mix well.

When the apricots become soft, remove from heat and refrigerate for 10 minutes.

In a bowl, whisk Greek yogurt and fresh cream together to form a smooth creamy mixture.

Combine the apricot and yogurt mixture together and enjoy with freshly baked macarons.

Recipe 6: Orange Blossom Macarons

The addition of citrus oranges gives macarons a very interesting tangy taste. If you like your macarons with a twist, this is the ultimate recipe to try because it uses dried orange zest to add a kick to it.

Yield: 12

Cooking Time: 40 minutes

List of Ingredients:

- Confectioner's sugar, 1 cup
- Orange essence, 2-4 drops
- Almond flour, ½ cup
- Orange food color, 2-4 drops
- 2 egg whites
- Dried orange zest, ½ teaspoons
- Powdered sugar, ½ cup

AAAAAAAAAAAAAAAAAAAAAAAAAAAAAAAAAAAAAAAAAAAAAAAAAAAAAA

Instructions:

Preheat the oven to 375 degrees.

Mix orange zest, almond flour and icing sugar in a food processor.

In a small bowl, whisk eggs on medium speed until fluffy.

Add sugar gradually and keep whisking to form a glossy mixture.

Stir in food color and essence and whisk for 5 seconds.

Combine the dried and wet mixture together and fold well using a spatula.

Using a piping cone, form round macarons from the batter.

Bake for about 20 minutes until golden brown.

Enjoy with your favorite dipping.

Recipe 7: Pineapple Macarons

If you like Mediterranean taste, you would love this recipe! Pineapples are known to be some of the most refreshing fruits out there. So it makes total sense to use them in macarons and enjoy their flavor.

Yield: 14

Cooking Time: 1hour 45minutes

List of Ingredients:

For Macarons

- Dried coconut flakes, 15 grams
- Yellow food color, 3-4 drops
- Finely grounded almonds, 15 grams
- Caster sugar, 50 grams
- Powdered icing sugar, 100 grams
- 2 egg whites

For Filling

- Pineapple puree (canned), 25 grams
- Icing sugar, 100 grams
- Coconut cream, 2 tablespoons

AAAAAAAAAAAAAAAAAAAAAAAAAAAAAAAAAAAAAAAAAAAAAAAAAAA

Instructions:

Preheat the oven to 160°C.

In a food processor, mix caster sugar, coconut flaks and almonds to form a powdery mixture.

In a small bowl, whisk eggs on medium speed.

Add icing sugar and whisk some more to form a glossy mixture.

Combine both mixtures together and fold well using a flat spatula.

Using a piping cone, make small round macarons from the batter.

Bake for about 20 minutes until golden brown.

For filling, whip coconut cream and icing sugar together.

Add pineapple puree and mix well.

Refrigerate for 15 minutes.

Sandwich the filling between two macarons and enjoy!

Chapter II - Divine Flavors

If you are bored with the basic macaron recipe and want to try some new flavors, give these recipes a try!

AAAAAAAAAAAAAAAAAAAAAAAAAAAAAAAAAAAAAAAAAAAAAAAAAAAAAA

Recipe 8: Oatmeal Macarons

Are you on a low-calorie diet? Include these low calorie oatmeal macarons in your diet chart and get rid of those pounds. In addition, the fiber you get from oatmeal will ensure you maintain a healthy digestive system.

Yield: 12

Cooking Time: 2 hours

List of Ingredients:

- Shortening, ½ cup
- Cocoa powder, ½ cup
- Skimmed milk, ½ cup
- Roasted oats, 2 ½ cups
- White sugar, 2 cups
- Unsweetened coconut flakes, ½ cup

AAAAAAAAAAAAAAAAAAAAAAAAAAAAAAAAAAAAAAAAAAAAAAAAAAAAA

Instructions:

Heat milk and shortening in a small saucepan over medium flame.

When the mixture starts simmering, add sugar and stir well.

When the sugar is completely dissolved, turn off the flame.

Stir in cocoa powder and coconut flakes and mix well.

Finally add roasted oatmeal and combine all the ingredients well.

Form small macarons from the mixture in a flat tray and cover with a foil.

Refrigerate for about 2 hours.

Enjoy chilled!

Recipe 9: Salted Caramel Macarons

If you don't have a sweet tooth, try this macaron recipe! It can be your perfect evening snack. It blends sweet with salt to give you delectable taste that you'll remember for days to come!

Yield: 34

Cooking Time: 1hour

List of Ingredients:

- Confectioner's sugar, 2 cups
- Grounded cinnamon, a pinch
- Almond flour, 1 cup
- Caster sugar, 2 ½ tablespoons
- 3 large eggs (only white)
- Cooking salt, ½ teaspoons
- For Salted Caramel Filling
- Unsalted butter, ½ cup
- Salted caramel, ½ cup
- Confectioner's sugar, 1 ½ cup
- Vanilla extract, 1 teaspoon

AA

Instructions:

Preheat the oven to 325°F.

In a small bowl, mix flour and confectioner's sugar using a food processor.

In another bowl, whisk egg whites on medium speed.

Stir in salt and caster sugar and whisk for 3 minutes.

Pour whisked eggs over the dried mixture and fold well using a spatula.

Set the batter aside for 10 minutes.

Fill the batter in a pipe cone and make sure there are no air bubbles left.

Grease a baking tray using greasing oil.

Make small cookies from the batter and sprinkle grounded cinnamon.

Bake the macarons for about 15 minutes in the preheated oven.

While the macarons are baking, start preparing for the salted caramel filling.

In a small bowl, beat butter until smooth.

Add confectioner's sugar and vanilla extract and mix well.

Finally add salted caramel and whisk for 2 minutes.

Take out the macarons from the oven when they turn golden brown.

Sandwich the salted caramel filling between two macarons and enjoy!

Recipe 10: Pistachio Macarons

Not only are these macarons extremely delicious but also very healthy from nutritional point of view. Pistachios are known to provide a wide array of health benefits, so why not enjoy them with delicious macarons?

Yield: 12

Cooking Time: 1hour

List of Ingredients:

- Grounded almonds, 1 ½ cups
- Pistachio nuts, grounded, ½ cup
- Icing sugar, 2 cups
- Green food color, 2-4 drops
- 4 large eggs, only white

Filling

- White chocolate, diced, 100 grams
- Heavy cream, 2 tablespoons

AAAAAAAAAAAAAAAAAAAAAAAAAAAAAAAAAAAAAAAAAAAAAAAAAAAAAA

Instructions:

In a food processor, grind pistachio and almonds together.

In a small bowl, whisk egg whites on medium speed.

Add icing sugar and food color and whisk on medium speed for 5 minutes.

Combine dry and wet mixture together and fold well.

Preheat oven to 130°C.

Form small macarons from the batter and bake for about 15 minutes.

While the macarons are baking, heat white chocolate and heavy cream in a saucepan.

Remove from heat when the chocolate is completely melted.

Refrigerate for about 40 minutes.

Enjoy pistachio macarons with white chocolate dip!

Recipe 11: Nut Choc Macarons

Filled with chocolate and coated with nuts, this macaron recipe is worth a try! The nuts and chocolate when mixed together create an irresistible taste that your guests will surely enjoy.

Yield: 15

Cooking Time: 1h 45min

List of Ingredients:

For Ganache

- Milk chocolate, good quality and finely chopped, 1 ½ oz.
- Kosher salt, a pinch
- Unsalted butter, 1 tablespoon
- Vanilla extract, ½ teaspoons
- Heavy cream, 1 tablespoon

For Macarons

- Whole almonds, grounded, ½ cup
- Food color (any), 2-4 drops
- Confectioner's sugar, 1 cup
- Almond extract, 1 teaspoon
- 2 large eggs, only white
- Caster sugar, 2 tablespoons
- Kosher salt, a pinch

AAAAAAAAAAAAAAAAAAAAAAAAAAAAAAAAAAAAAAAAAAAAAAAAAAAAA

Instructions:

Preheat the oven to 325°F.

In a small bowl, mix grounded almonds and confectioner's sugar using a food processor.

In another bowl, whisk egg whites on medium speed.

Stir in salt, almond extract, food color and caster sugar and whisk for 3 minutes.

Pour whisked eggs over the dried mixture and fold well using a spatula.

Set the batter aside for 10 minutes.

Make small round cookies from the batter and bake for about 15 minutes until golden brown.

Meanwhile, start preparing for the filling.

In a small saucepan, heat chocolate chunks and butter together over small flame.

When the ingredients are completely melted, add cream, salt and vanilla extract and stir well.

Remove from heat and refrigerate for 30 minutes.

Take out the macarons from the oven and enjoy with the chilled ganche.

Recipe 12: Vanilla Macarons

Everyone likes vanilla flavor. Just a little addition of vanilla extract can give regular macarons a whole new dimension. The almonds and Swiss butter cream give this recipe the edge.

Yield: 10

Cooking Time: 2hours

List of Ingredients:

- Whole almonds, diced, ½ cup
- Food color, 2-4 drops
- Confectioner's sugar, 1 cup
- Vanilla bean seeds, 1 teaspoon
- 2 large eggs, only white
- Caster sugar, ½ cup
- Swiss butter cream, ½ cup

AAAAAAAAAAAAAAAAAAAAAAAAAAAAAAAAAAAAAAAAAAAAAAAAAAAAAAA

Instructions:

Preheat oven to 350 degrees.

In a food processor, blend confectioner's sugar and diced almonds together to form powdery mixture.

In a small bowl, whisk egg whites until smooth.

Add vanilla seeds and food color and whisk on medium speed for 3 minutes.

Combine dry and wet mixture together.

Mix well using a flat spatula.

Grease a baking tray using cooking oil.

Form small macarons form the batter using a pipe cone.

Bake for about 15-20 minutes until golden brown.

Coat the baked macarons with butter cream and refrigerate for 1 hour.

Enjoy chilled!

Recipe 13: Mocha Macarons

These coffee-flavored macarons can be your daily dose of caffeine. If you want to cut down on your caffeine intake, give this recipe a try. The mocha is a great way to wake you up in the morning.

Yield: 8

Cooking Time: 1h 40min

List of Ingredients:

- Confectioners' sugar, 1 ½ cups
- Cooking salt, 1 teaspoon
- Hazelnuts, toasted, ½ cup
- 3 large eggs, only white
- Dutch cocoa powder, 2 ½ tablespoons
- Mocha Filling
- Milk chocolate, diced, 4 oz.
- Espresso powder, 1 tablespoon
- Heavy cream, ¾ cup

AAAAAAAAAAAAAAAAAAAAAAAAAAAAAAAAAAAAAAAAAAAAAAAAAAAAAAA

Instructions:

Preheat the oven to 325°F.

Grind confectioner's sugar, toasted hazelnuts and cocoa powder in a food processor.

In a small bowl, whisk eggs over medium speed.

Add salt and whisk some more.

Combine the dried and wet mixture together and fold well using a spatula.

Grease a baking tray using cooking oil.

Make small macarons from the batter and bake for about 15-20 minutes until golden brown.

While the macarons are baking, heat heavy cream and chocolate in a sauce pan.

When the chocolate is completely melted, add instant espresso powder and stir well.

Remove the filling from heat and refrigerate for 30 minutes.

Enjoy crunchy macarons with mocha dip!

Chapter III - Macarons Madness across the Globe

Although macarons is basically a French confection, but you know they say taste knows no border. Over the years, macarons have become a part of every cuisine. Almost every country in the world has its own version of macarons. In this section, you will enjoy macaron recipes from 8 cuisines. So here we go:

AAAAAAAAAAAAAAAAAAAAAAAAAAAAAAAAAAAAAAAAAAAAAAAAAAAAAA

Recipe 14: German Coconut Macaron

Are you fond of cookies? Try these crispy tropical macarons all the way from Deutschland! But it doesn't matter where you reside at the end of the day, you'll find these delicious.

Yield: 36

Cooking Time: 20minutes

List of Ingredients:

- Coconut flakes, toasted, 2 ½ cups
- Almond extract, ½ teaspoons
- 4 large eggs, only white
- White sugar, ¾ cup
- Cinnamon, finely grounded, 1 teaspoon

AAAAAAAAAAAAAAAAAAAAAAAAAAAAAAAAAAAAAAAAAAAAAAAAAAAAA

Instructions:

Preheat the oven to 250 degrees.

In a large bowl, whisk eggs on medium speed until fluffy.

Add sugar, extract and cinnamon and keep mixing.

When the mixture reaches a thick consistency, stir in coconut flakes.

Use a flat spatula to mix all the ingredients well.

Grease a flat baking tray and form cookies from the batter.

Bake macarons for about 15 minutes until golden brown.

Enjoy with your favorite filling!

Recipe 15: Basic French Macarons

Being an integral part of French cuisine, you can find a ton of variants of French macarons. But this is the very basic recipe of French macarons which are bite sized almond cookies. Enjoy with your choice of filling!

Yield: 8

Cooking Time: 2h 10min

List of Ingredients:

- 3 egg whites
- Confectioner's sugar, 1 ½ cups
- Almonds, finely chopped, 1 cup
- White sugar, ½ cup

AAAAAAAAAAAAAAAAAAAAAAAAAAAAAAAAAAAAAAAAAAAAAAAAAAAAAAAAAA

Instructions:

Preheat oven to 285oF.

In a small bowl mix grounded almonds and confectionary sugar together.

In another bowl, beat egg whites until frothy.

Add white sugar and whisk some more until the mixture is smooth and firm.

Stir in almond mixture and beat well to form a smooth, creamy batter.

Line a baking tray with aluminum foil and grease using cooking oil.

Spread the batter in small circles, using a spatula or paper cone.

Bake for about 10-15minutes until the cookies are golden brown.

Sandwich your favorite filling between two cookies and enjoy!

Recipe 16: Thai Tea Macarons

These iced tea macarons are perfect for hot sunny days. Enjoy with your favorite chiller and beat the heat. These are favorites in regions where the weather is warm.

Yield: 10

Cooking Time: 1hour

List of Ingredients:

- Macaron Shells
- Egg white, 150 grams
- Food color (red and yellow), 3-4 drops
- Caster sugar, 70 grams
- Almonds, finely grounded, 120 grams
- Icing sugar, 250 grams

For Filling

- Thai iced tea, 5 tea bags
- Unsalted butter, refrigerated and diced in small cubes, 40 grams
- Distilled water, 150ml
- Condensed milk (sweetened), 1 tablespoon
- Whipped cream, 20 grams
- White chocolate, 50 grams

AAAAAAAAAAAAAAAAAAAAAAAAAAAAAAAAAAAAAAAAAAAAAAAAAAAAAA

Instructions:

Preheat the oven to 180 degrees.

In a small bowl, mix grounded almonds and icing sugar together and set aside.

In another bowl, whisk egg on medium speed.

Stir in salt and caster sugar and whisk on high speed to blend all the ingredients thoroughly.

Make sure the mixture is consistent and stiff.

Finally, add the dried almond mixture and food color to whisked eggs.

Beat a little more to make a creamy and stiff batter.

Line a baking tray with aluminum foil and grease with cooking oil.

Using a piping bag, spread the batter in the form of small cookies.

Make sure the batter is air free.

Put the tray in the oven and bake for 20 minutes.

While the macarons are in making, start preparing for the filling.

Heat water on small flame with iced tea bags in it.

When the mixture reaches a thick consistency, add condensed milk.

Bring the mixture to boil.

In another pan, melt white chocolate and butter together.

Add chocolate mixture to the iced tea mixture.

Let the filling cool down.

Fill the baked macaron shells with delicious ganache and enjoy!

Recipe 17: Indian Thoothukudi Macarons

This macaron recipe is immensely popular in South India and if you want an instant sugar rush, give this recipe a try. These macarons are rarely found at bakeries in the West, so it's good to know how to make them.

Yield: 20

List of Ingredients:

- 3 large eggs, only white part
- Cashew nuts, finely grounded, 100 grams
- White sugar, 80 grams

AAAAAAAAAAAAAAAAAAAAAAAAAAAAAAAAAAAAAAAAAAAAAAAAAAAAAAAA

Instructions:

Preheat the oven to 180 degrees.

In a small bowl whisk egg whites using a hand beater.

Add sugar and whisk for about 5 minutes until the mixture is consistent and stiff.

At this point, stir in powdered cashew nuts and whisk for about 3 minutes

Set the batter aside for about 5 minutes.

Grease a baking tray using cooking oil.

Form small cookies from the batter using a pipe cone or tablespoon.

Bake the cookies for about 15 minutes until fully done.

Serve cashew macarons with your favorite dipping.

Recipe 18: Mexican Dulce De Leche Macarons

Mexican food is famous for its spicy taste. Now that you have tried French macarons, try these spiced macarons with a local Mexican confection Dulce De Leche.

Yield: 8

Cooking Time: 1hour

List of Ingredients:

For Macarons

- 4 egg whites
- Distilled water, 50g
- White sugar, 35g
- Cinnamon, ½ teaspoons
- Almonds, finely grounded, 150g
- Coffee powder, 7g
- Grounded sugar, 150g
- Cocoa powder, 1 teaspoon
- Vanilla extract, 1 ½ teaspoons

For Filling

- Condensed milk, sweetened, 1 small can

AAAAAAAAAAAAAAAAAAAAAAAAAAAAAAAAAAAAAAAAAAAAAAAAAAAA

Instructions:

Preheat the oven to 300°F.

Heat the water over medium flame and stir in white sugar.

Let the mixture come to boil.

In a small bowl whisk eggs until firm and fluffy.

Add powdered sugar and whisk some more.

Pour the sugar syrup into whisked eggs and whisk on high speed.

Add cinnamon, grounded almond, cocoa powder and coffee to the mixture and mix well.

Make sure the batter is firm and consistent.

Fill paper cone with the batter and line a baking tray with aluminum foil.

Make small cookies from the batter using the paper cone and let them dry.

Bake the macarons for about 15 minutes until golden brown.

While the macarons are cooking, prepare the filling.

Pour the condensed milk in a large flat bowl and microwave for about 5 minutes.

Take out the baked macarons from the oven and fill them with the caramelized condensed milk!

Recipe 19: Nutty Brazilian Macarons

This flourless desert is perfect if you are craving for something nutty and crispy. Plus, if you are on diet, this low calorie treat is perfect for you. It's healthy and filling at the same time.

Yield: 18

Cooking Time: 2 days

List of Ingredients:

- Instant oats, 2 cups
- Brazilian nuts, coarsely chopped, ½ cup
- White sugar, ½ cup
- 1 large egg
- Orange zest, 2 teaspoons
- Vegetable oil, ¾ cup
- Cooking salt, ¾ teaspoons

AAAAAAAAAAAAAAAAAAAAAAAAAAAAAAAAAAAAAAAAAAAAAAAAAAAAAAAA

Instructions:

In a salad bowl mix oats with shredded orange zest, salt and sugar.

Toss all the ingredients well and cover with a lid.

Refrigerate overnight.

Take out the mixture from the refrigerator and allow it to set on room temperature.

Preheat the oven to 300 degrees.

In a small bowl whisk egg and add coarsely chopped nuts.

Add the refrigerated mixture to whisked egg and blend all the ingredients well.

Using a tablespoon, make small cookies from the batter and spread on a flat baking tray.

Bake for about 15 minutes and you are done

Recipe 20: Italian Meringue Macarons

If you have never tried macarons before, start with Italian macarons. The recipe is really easy and you can enjoy it with your favorite filling!

Yield: 12

Cooking Time: 1hour

List of Ingredients:

For Macarons

- Almond flour, 100g
- Icing sugar, 100g

For Meringue

- Egg whites (dehydrated), 1 egg
- White Sugar, 70g
- Distilled water, 20ml
- Egg white, 20g

AAAAAAAAAAAAAAAAAAAAAAAAAAAAAAAAAAAAAAAAAAAAAAAAAAAAA

Instructions:

Preheat the oven to 170°C.

In a small bowl mix almond flour and icing sugar together and set aside.

Heat water over medium flame and bring it to boil.

Stir in white sugar, let it fully dissolve in the water and turn off the flame.

In a small bowl whip dried and wet egg whites together.

Slowly add sugar syrup to whipped eggs and keep whisking.

Make sure the mixture is firm and frothy.

Now add this mixture to the powdered mixture.

Mix well with a spatula and make sure there are no air bubbles left.

Using a paper cone, make small round macarons in the baking tray.

Put the tray in oven and bake for about 20minutes until golden brown.

Take out the tray and there you are!

Recipe 21: Scottish Macarons

If you are a coconut lover, you will love this delectable treat! Scottish macaron bars are totally irresistible. They have great taste and the dark chocolate gives them a rich taste. Give this recipe a try and see for yourself.

Yield: 12

Cooking Time: 5hours

List of Ingredients:

- Potato, 4 ounces
- Coconut, finely grated (for coating)
- Powdered sugar, 1 pound
- Dark Chocolate, for dipping

AAAAAAAAAAAAAAAAAAAAAAAAAAAAAAAAAAAAAAAAAAAAAAAAAAAAAAAAAA

Instructions:

In a large pan boil potatoes.

Peel and mash boiled potatoes.

Add half cup of powdered sugar to mashed potatoes and mix well.

Keep adding sugar gradually and mixing well.

Use a flat spatula to mix the ingredients.

When the batter becomes consistent and fondant-like, make small balls and flatten them.

Refrigerate the macarons for 4 hours.

Preheat the oven to 280 degrees and roast shredded coconut for 5 minutes.

Allow the roasted coconut to cool down.

Melt dark chocolate in a flat bowl and take out macaron cookies from the refrigerator.

Dip the cookies in molten chocolate and coat with roasted coconuts.

Allow the chocolate coating to harden before serving.

Enjoy!

Recipe 22: Turkish Date Macaron

Date is one of the integral ingredients of Turkish deserts. The addition of date gives macarons a whole new dimension. Give this recipe a try!

Yield: 12

Cooking Time: 30minutes

List of Ingredients:

- Coconut, 1 cup
- Vanilla extract, ½ teaspoons
- Dates, finely diced, ½ cup
- 1 egg
- Cooking salt, ¼ teaspoons
- White sugar, ½ cup
- Nuts (of your choice), coarsely chopped, ½ cup

AAAAAAAAAAAAAAAAAAAAAAAAAAAAAAAAAAAAAAAAAAAA/\/\/\/\AAAAAAAAAAA

Instructions:

Preheat the oven to 300 degrees.

In a small bowl whisk eggs until fluffy.

Stir in salt and vanilla extract and whisk some more.

In another bowl, mix nuts, sugar, diced dates and coconut together.

Add the dried mixture to whisked eggs and whisk for 5 minutes.

Spread the batter on the baking tray in the form of small cookies.

Bake for around 15 minutes until golden brown and fully done.

Enjoy with tea or coffee!

Chapter IV - Macron-ish Deserts

Now that you know the basic recipe of macarons, let's take the macaron mania one step further. Use the basic macaron recipe to make these delicious deserts!

AAAAAAAAAAAAAAAAAAAAAAAAAAAAAAAAAAAAAAAAAAAAAAAAAAAA

Recipe 23: Macaron Pudding

This recipe makes a perfect midnight snack! Not only it's easy to make but also very filling and healthy. This recipe will put regular pudding on hold because once you try this, you won't like the regular version anymore.

Yield: 4

Cooking Time: 20minutes

List of Ingredients:

- Macarons (of your choice), 250 grams
- Pudding moulds
- Corn flour, 65 grams
- Almond extract, 3tbsp
- Vanilla sugar, 3 sachets
- Double cream, 450 ml
- White sugar, 2 ½ tablespoons
- Fat milk, 450 ml

AAAAAAAAAAAAAAAAAAAAAAAAAAAAAAAAAAAAAAAAAAAAAAAAAAAAAAA

Instructions:

Crush the macarons in a small bowl and set aside.

In a sauce pan, heat 400 ml of fattened milk and cream together.

Keep the flame low.

In another small bowl, toss vanilla sugar and white sugar together.

Pour the remaining milk into the mixture and blend well.

Add macaron crumbles to the cream and milk mixture and stir well.

When the macarons are fully dissolved and the mixture starts bubbling, stir in the corn flour mixture.

Keep stirring, so that there are no lumps left.

When the mixture reaches a thick consistency, turn off the flame.

Pour the pudding into moulds and cover with foil.

Refrigerate for 3-4 hours.

Enjoy chilled.

Recipe 24: Cherry Macaron Pie

Enthrall your taste buds with this delicious chocolate pie, topped with cherries and filled with crunchy macarons. It doesn't get any better than this recipe because it has coconut, chocolate, and cherries!

Yield: 5

Cooking Time: 30minutes

List of Ingredients:

- Cherry pie filling, 1 small can
- Pie crust (chocolate flavor, 10 inch
- Chocolate chips, ½ cup

For Filling

- Coconut flakes, 1 ½ cups
- Chocolate chips, ½ cup, for toping
- Condensed milk, 1 small can

AAAAAAAAAAAAAAAAAAAAAAAAAAAAAAAAAAAAAAAAAAAAAAAAAAAA

Instructions:

Preheat oven to 350 degrees.

In a flat tray spread coconut flakes, ¾ cup condensed milk and chocolate chips.

Cover the mixture with pie crust.

Bake the macaron pie crust for about 20 minutes.

In a sauce pan, add chocolate chips and the remaining condensed milk.

Heat the ingredients over medium flame until the chocolate chips are fully melted.

Pour the melted mixture over the macaron pie and allow cooling on room temperature.

Recipe 25: Coconut Macaron Waffles

Crispy macaron waffles on the outside filled with coconut and chocolate is all you need to give your day a perfect start. This recipe creates an item that's filling and delicious.

Yield: 1

Cooking Time: 20 minutes

List of Ingredients:

- Grounded flax, 1 tablespoon (dissolved in 2tbsp distilled water)
- Coconut flakes, shredded and roasted (for topping)
- Whipped cream, for coating
- Quinoa flour, ¾ cup
- Coconut extract, ½ teaspoons
- Coconut (unsweetened), finely shredded, 2 ½ tablespoons
- Vanilla extract, ½ teaspoons
- Almond meal, 2 tablespoons
- Coconut milk, ½ cup + ¾ tablespoons
- Baking powder, ½ teaspoons
- Cooking salt, ½ teaspoons

- Cinnamon, finely grounded, ½ teaspoons

For Coffee Dip

- Instant hot coffee, ¾ tablespoons
- Raw honey or maple syrup, ½ tablespoons
- Coconut oil, ¾ tablespoons
- Chocolate chips, 1 tablespoon
- Cocoa powder (good quality), 1 tablespoon

AAAAAAAAAAAAAAAAAAAAAAAAAAAAAAAAAAAAAAAAAAAAAAAAAAAAAAAAA

Instructions:

Preheat the waffle grill.

In a small bowl, mix quinoa flour and unsweetened shredded coconut.

Stir in baking powder, salt, almond meal and grounded cinnamon.

Mix all the ingredients well and set aside.

In another small bowl, mix coconut milk, vanilla extract, coconut milk and coconut extract.

Add flax to the mixture and blend well.

Stir in the dried mixture and mix thoroughly.

Cook macarons on the preheated waffle iron.

While the macarons are on the grill, mix coconut oil and coffee in a small bowl.

Add cocoa powder and maple syrup and blend well.

Sprinkle chocolate chips and set the dip aside.

Turn off the grill when the macaron waffles turn golden brown.

Dip the macaron waffles in the coffee syrup,

Enjoy warm!

Recipe 26: Macaron Nest

This little treat is perfect for traditions like Easter and Christmas. Buttery macaron cookies covered in a coconut nest are totally irresistible. They create a lively mood during the holidays because everyone can enjoy them.

Yield: 36

Cooking Time: 1hour

List of Ingredients:

- All-purpose flour, 1 ½ cups
- Peanuts (preferably chocolate coated), 1 cup
- Baking powder, 1 tablespoon
- Red and yellow food color, 2-3 drops
- Cooking salt, ½ teaspoons
- Unsweetened coconut flakes, 1 ½ cups
- Unsalted butter, ½ cup
- Vanilla extract, ½ teaspoons
- Cream cheese, 8 oz.
- White sugar, 1 ½ cup

AAAAAAAAAAAAAAAAAAAAAAAAAAAAAAAAAAAAAAAAAAAAAAAAAAAAA

Instructions:

Preheat oven to 325 degrees.

In a small bowl, toss flour, cooking salt and baking powder together.

In another bowl, whip cream cheese and butter together.

Add sugar and mix well.

Stir on the powdered mixture and blend all the ingredients well to form a creamy batter.

Set the batter aside.

Divide the shredded coconut into three parts.

Add red color to one part, yellow to the second and leave the remaining one plain.

Mix colored and plain coconut flakes together and set aside.

Form small macaron balls from the batter and roll them over the shredded coconut.

Put 1 chocolate coated peanut in the center of each macaron.

Bake the macarons for about 15 minutes, until golden brown.

Allow cooling on room temperature before serving.

Recipe 27: Topical Macaron Tart

The Macaron tart makes an amazing tea-time and part desert. You can preserve it an airtight container and enjoy it for days. It will come out as fresh as when you made it.

Yield: 6

Cooking Time: 2hr

List of Ingredients:

- Instant pastry dough, ½ cup
- 3 large eggs
- Icing sugar, for coating
- Cater sugar, finely grounded, 8 oz.
- Grounded cinnamon, 1 teaspoon
- Unsalted butter, melted, 1 stick + 1 tablespoon
- Unsweetened coconut, finely shredded, 5 oz.

∧∧

Instructions:

Prepare the pastry dough (following the instructions on the packet) and refrigerate for 30 minutes to set the dough.

Preheat the oven to 325 degrees.

In a small bowl whisk eggs on medium speed until fluffy.

Add grounded caster sugar and grounded cinnamon and whisk some more.

Finally add shredded coconut and molten butter to the mixture and blend well.

Pour the mixture over refrigerated pastry dough and put it in the preheated oven.

Let it bake for 40 minutes until golden brown.

Remove the macaron tart from the oven and allow cooling down.

Coat with icing sugar before serving.

Recipe 28: Macaron Cake

Spongy cake topped with crunchy macarons makes a perfect desert for birthdays and special occasions. The next time you're having a birthday party at your place, try this new cake on for size.

Yield: 12

Cooking Time: 45minutes

List of Ingredients:

- Molten butter (unsalted), for greasing
- Raspberry jam, ¾ cups
- Unsalted butter, 80 grams
- Vanilla essence, 1 teaspoon
- Caster sugar, ¾ cup
- Milk, ½ cup
- 3 eggs, only yolk
- Baking powder, 2 ½ teaspoons
- 6-7 macarons, for topping

AAAAAAAAAAAAAAAAAAAAAAAAAAAAAAAAAAAAAAAAAAAAAAAAAAAAAAA

Instructions:

Preheat oven to 180°C.

In a sauce pan, melt butter over small flame.

When the butter is fully melted, add milk and egg yolks and whisk well.

Add sugar, baking powder and vanilla essence and mix all the ingredients well.

Finally add flour and fold the cake batter with a spatula.

When the batter is lump free and consistent, remove from the heat.

Transfer the batter into a baking tray, greased with melted butter.

Top the batter with raspberry jam and put it in the oven.

Bake for about half an hour.

Check the doneness of the cake using a knife.

Take out the cake when it's fully done.

Top with crumbled macarons and enjoy.

Recipe 29: Macaron Ice-cream

Want to try a whole new ice-cream flavor? Give this recipe a try and beat the heat the macaron-ish way! We bet that you've never had ice cream that tastes so good and has the flavor of macarons.

Yield: 12

Cooking Time: 3 hours

List of Ingredients:

- Heavy cream, whipped, 2 cups
- Ice cream maker
- Half and half, 2 cups
- Air tight container
- White sugar, 1 cup
- Sprinkles, for topping
- Vanilla extract, 1 teaspoon
- Macarons (any flavor of your choice), 4-5 pieces

AAAAAAAAAAAAAAAAAAAAAAAAAAAAAAAAAAAAAAAAAAAAAAAAAAAAAA

Instructions:

Crush the macarons in a small bowl and set aside.

In another bowl, combine whisked cream and half and half together.

Stir in sugar and vanilla extract and mix until the mixture reaches a thick consistency,

Now pour the batter into the ice cream maker and blend on medium speed for about 15 minutes.

Transfer the mixture into the airtight container and refrigerate for 3 hours.

Take out the macaron ice cream from the freezer and top with colorful sprinkles before serving!

About the Author

Molly Mills always knew she wanted to feed people delicious food for a living. Being the oldest child with three younger brothers, Molly learned to prepare meals at an early age to help out her busy parents. She just seemed to know what spice went with which meat and how to make sauces that would dress up the blandest of pastas. Her creativity in the kitchen was a blessing to a family where money was tight and making new meals every day was a challenge.

Molly was also a gifted athlete as well as chef and secured a Lacrosse scholarship to Syracuse University. This was a blessing to her family as she was the first to go to college and at little cost to her parents. She took full advantage of her college education and earned a business degree. When she graduated, she joined her culinary skills and business acumen into a successful catering business. She wrote her first e-book after a customer asked if she could pay for several of her recipes. This sparked the entrepreneurial spirit in Mills and she thought if one person wanted them, then why not share the recipes with the world!

Molly lives near her family's home with her husband and three children and still cooks for her family every chance she gets. She plays Lacrosse with a local team made up of her old teammates from college and there are always some tasty nibbles on the ready after each game.

Don't Miss Out!

Scan the QR-Code below and you can sign up to receive emails whenever Molly Mills publishes a new book. There's no charge and no obligation.

Sign Me Up

https://molly.gr8.com

Printed in Great Britain
by Amazon